HEAVEN, HELL AND OTHER PLACES

a film about Emanuel Swedenborg

THE SWEDENBORG SOCIETY

Apocalypsis
Revelata

Foreword
Philip Makatrewicz

This DVD is intended to introduce the scientist and mystic Emanuel Swedenborg to a wider audience. Quite fittingly, I came to this project knowing precious little about the man himself. Indeed, that was producer, Stephen McNeilly's premise—expose a curious mind to this rather marginal historical figure and see what happened. That one of my favourite writers, Jorge Luis Borges, labelled Swedenborg 'the most interesting man in recorded history' suggested that a colourful journey lay ahead.

As I began my research, speaking to the wise heads that feature in the documentary, it became clear that Swedenborg's story offers something for everyone. The sceptic can hardly turn his nose up at Swedenborg's multifarious accomplishments in the tangible, material world of science and engineering. It is difficult to dismiss an intellect lively enough to tackle all the grand questions of the age—his *Principia* was an attempt to explain how a finite, mechanistic world came to being from the infinite. The same intellect would also devote time to designing prototypes of a flying machine, mapping the human brain, making advances in crystallography and figuring out how to transport eight Swedish boats over fifteen miles of land so the navy could launch a surprise attack on Norway.

The agnostic can marvel at the scope and completeness of his visions, and find spiritual nourishment in the insights gleaned from his reports of inter-dimensional travels. He appealed to poets—Blake, Coleridge, Baudelaire—and no wonder. There is enough strangeness in his writing to stir the weariest of imaginations, and in all the vast volumes chronicling

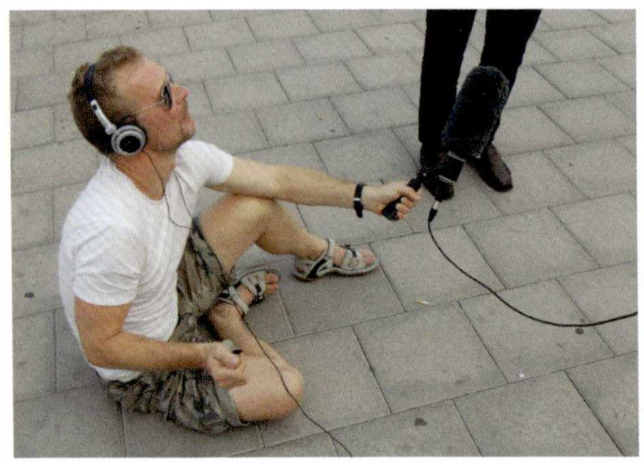

INSANE!
TELE2

encounters with angels and devils and souls on the other side, enough to keep that imagination engaged for a very long time. In the material realm, breath experiments, hypnagogia, clairvoyance, mediumship and esoteric eroticism are just some of the elements that make the narrative of his waking life equally compelling.

For the convert, a whole creed becomes available, one that has given many people around the world strength and guidance. If you wished somehow to quantify the value of his teachings, a glance at the humanitarian achievements of eminent Swedenborgians would make even the most vitriolic New Atheist struggle to object. His followers made vital contributions to the abolition of slavery, as well as political and educational reform, confirming that Swedenborg's teachings transcended their time and promoted many of the benevolent, egalitarian ideas we are lucky enough to take for granted today.

Whatever the reality of his experiences, Swedenborg's conduct bore out their benefits. As per his own dictum, here was a man who shone the light of his love outwards, not inwards. When his concern was for the material world, he craved fame and recognition. When his gaze shifted to the spiritual plane, he asked for nothing, wanted for nothing, and lived a kind, humble and busy life. In his dealings with others he was palpably sane, staying active in public and political affairs to prove it. If madness this was, I would like a bottle of it for myself.

But it is not for me to make up your mind; let the facts speak for themselves. It is my hope that this documentary, as well as seducing you with the stunning visuals of co-directors Jacob Cartwright and Nick Jordan, will provide enough of them for you to decide whether this remarkable man merits any more of your attention. I only wish you find as much pleasure in your journey as I found in mine.

Introducing Swedenborg
Gary Lachman

The Swedish scientist, traveller, statesman, and religious philosopher
Emanuel Swedenborg—to name only a few of his careers—is one of
the most fascinating individuals in the Western intellectual and spiritual
traditions. He is also, unfortunately, one of the least understood. If people
know of Swedenborg at all, it is usually because of his connection with the
poet William Blake, who was a follower of Swedenborg but took argument
with him in works like *The Marriage of Heaven and Hell*. Or they may
know of Swedenborg because of his remarkable psychic powers, chronicled
in histories of the occult and paranormal. Not only did Swedenborg
accurately predict the time and day of his death—29 March 1772—he
also was somehow conscious of a fire that broke out in Stockholm when
he was at a dinner party in another town, some three hundred miles away.
Swedenborg amazed the dinner guests as he reported on the spread and
eventual halt of the blaze, and when the news of it reached them a few days
later—this was some centuries before the mobile phone or internet—they
discovered that Swedenborg had been correct. Yet Blake was only one of
the many thinkers, artists and writers influenced by Swedenborg; a full
list would include, among others, figures such as Ralph Waldo Emerson,
Charles Baudelaire, August Strindberg, Honoré de Balzac and Jorge Luis
Borges. And his psychic abilities extended far beyond clairvoyance, into
interplanetary travel and visits to heaven and hell, where he conversed with
angels and devils and other strange beings.

Swedenborg was born in Stockholm in 1688 into a very religious
family—his father was ordained a bishop—but early on he showed a

more practical and scientific turn of mind. Swedenborg began his career as an engineer, and some of his early accomplishments include designing the locks on the Trollhättan Canal; devising Sweden's first saltworks; and moving the Swedish navy some fifteen miles across land during a war with Norway. In his travels Swedenborg reported on scientific developments across Europe and helped to start the first Swedish scientific journal, filling its pages with articles on metallurgy and mechanics. He also just missed winning the contest to solve the problem of ascertaining longitude at sea, losing out to the British clockmaker John Harrison. But although he showed engineering genius, Swedenborg's true interest—his 'true affection', he would say—was more speculative and philosophical, and for much of his adult life Swedenborg focused his considerable intellectual powers on questions of cosmology, physics, anatomy, the brain, and those perennial mysteries, life and death. While fulfilling his obligations as Swedish Assessor of Mines—not to mention his responsibilities as a member of the Swedish Diet—Swedenborg's synthesis of and ruminations on the cutting-edge science of his time led to discoveries in galaxy formation, brain physiology, anatomy, and such modern concepts as pulsars, neurons, split-brain theory, and the anthropic principle. Swedenborg's countryman, the Nobel Prize winning scientist Svante Arrhenius, argued that among many other insights Swedenborg knew that our galaxy was only one of thousands, and that these 'island universes' themselves are part of a vast chain forming enormous stellar systems, something that was confirmed in recent times via the Hubble Space Telescope.

Yet although Swedenborg's scientific and engineering achievements are enough to warrant accolades as the 'Swedish Da Vinci', Swedenborg's remarkably prolific life did not end there. His poetry and his more than likely passing involvement in political espionage can only be alluded to here —I touch on them in my book *Into the Interior: Discovering Swedenborg*— but what grips our attention in an already gripping biography is the remarkable 'spiritual crisis' Swedenborg underwent in his mid-fifties. Having devoted his energies to discovering the 'seat of the soul' in the human body—and directing his attentions at the brain's mysterious pineal

gland, a humble organ whose precise function still eludes us—Swedenborg plunged into a study of the occult sciences and practices held in high esteem at the time. Through Kabbala, meditation, and a system of erotic exercises deriving from the Moravians and followers of Sabbatai Zevi, the 'false messiah', Swedenborg trained himself to enter prolonged periods of altered consciousness. One result of this is his fascinating *Dream Diary*, in which his analysis of the symbolic value of dreams predates Freud and Jung by a century and a half. Another was his profound intimacy with the hypnagogic state, a twilit, 'half-dream' realm we enter in between sleeping and waking. It was while hovering in this liminal consciousness—one explored by other, later seers, such as Rudolf Steiner and CG Jung—that Swedenborg had an experience that changed his life.

On 6 April 1744, while living in London, Swedenborg was visited by Christ. He had reached a dead end in his scientific work, and Christ had come to tell him to abandon it and devote himself to an even greater task: that of discovering the true meaning of Scripture. Swedenborg accepted the challenge and developed a symbolic way of reading the Bible that would have an impact on Western consciousness far beyond theology. It was through this new, analogical reading of Scripture, which jettisoned simplistic, literal interpretations, that Swedenborg devised the notion of correspondences, the idea that the elements of the physical world—mountains, flowers, stars, and so on—have a direct link with the higher, spiritual world. Although not entirely new—the ancient Hermetic dictum 'as above, so below' says as much—Swedenborg's insight would form the basis for Symbolism, one of the most important literary and art movements of the nineteenth century, responsible, among other things, for Wagner's operas and Mallarmé's poetry. More immediately, however, Swedenborg's accounts of his journeys to heaven, hell and other places, like the intermediary realm he called the 'spirit world', spelled out in homely parables the parallels between life on this earthly plane and events in these other spheres. Through his matter-of-fact reports on conditions in the afterworlds, Swedenborg showed how our actions here and now reflect our relation to the Divine. Yet these higher worlds were no allegorical

Swedenborgsgatan
kv. Fatbursbrunnen
12 - 10

Swedenborgsgatan
9-13

abstractions, and readers of Swedenborg's *Heaven and Hell* and *Conjugial Love*, one of his last books, encountered a very robust reality. Indeed, some of Swedenborg's last pronouncements on the social conditions of heaven—where, among other pursuits, angels engage in continuous and mutually satisfying lovemaking—make it seem infinitely more vital than what passes for life now. His hell, on the other hand, is more graphic than the latest HD horror film.

Yet Swedenborg was no woolly mystic, avoiding greasy flesh and blood in favour of some more ethereal existence. If his head was in the celestial clouds, his feet were planted firmly on the ground. Swedenborg's visions were not aimed at sidestepping our mundane duties, but at showing their link to a wider reality. In many ways his teaching boils down to the sobering admonition to 'Do the good that you know,' whether it is the washing up or taking out the rubbish. Hell, as the playwright Bernard Shaw, a reader of Swedenborg, knew, is a place of idleness, while heaven is the home of the 'masters of reality'. With any luck this film will introduce its viewers to a man who mastered reality in more worlds than one.

Afterword
Stephen McNeilly

This documentary has been a long time in the making.

First proposed in 2005, with ongoing discussions during 2006–2007, it gained significant momentum the following year in anticipation of the Swedenborg Society's bicentenary (2010). With the funding secured soon after, an itinerary was then drafted and key personnel selected: Jacob Cartwright, Nick Jordan, Philip Makatrewicz and myself, the four of us working in close collaboration, sharing thoughts and methods, selecting locations and themes.

My overriding memory of this early period is of many preliminary discussions and debates i.e. whether to situate Swedenborg within a broad historical context or to follow the idiosyncratic train of his own thinking. It is fair to say any number of films might have emerged, and hopefully some of these still will. In the end we sought to make him accessible, to bring him closer, approachable even, as a thinker giving shape to the modern world and also as a man whose life is still of interest today.

Filming itself finally began in the summer of 2009, and on three separate locations: Swedenborg's hometown Stockholm, where he owned property and attended the Swedish House of Nobles; Uppsala, the site of his study and final resting place; and London, the city of his visions, where he published and finally died. The final edit was signed off in early 2010, ready for its premiere screening at Swedenborg House on April 8th. Without a doubt a much longer film could easily have been made. The shorter, broadcast-friendly length however was chosen to give the film greater focus and accessibility.

biljett
Onsd
0-6
Boende
Sö
KÖP
TIDNINGEN
HÄR
KÖP
TIDNINGEN
HÄR
KÖP
TIDNINGEN
HÄR
KÖP
TIDNINGEN
HÄR
KÖP
TIDNINGEN
HÄR
Ladda ditt
kontantkort
här!
djuice
halebop
TANGO
TELIA
Vodafone
allas
Baka
PLAZA
CHARLOTTE
DEN SVENSKA GRÄDDGLASSENS
SiA
GLASS
DIPLO
SiA
GLASS

JCDecaux
sloggi
HOT HIPS
NOW IN COTTON
FOR THE FIRST TIME ON EARTH
www.sloggi.com

The list of people, friends and organizations who have aided us in the production of this film is a long one. Special mention must first go to the Board of Trustees of the Swedenborg Society (Michael Hiller in particular) for their support and encouragement, and continued patience. Further gratitude is also extended Annika Fundin, Lars Bergquist, Gary Lachman, Devin Zuber, and Richard Lines for their time and knowledge, and for agreeing to appear in the film. For their kindness and generosity during our stay in Stockholm, our sincere gratitude goes to Goran Applegren and Susanna Akerman-Hjern.

Acknowledgements are also due to Helene Winberg at Skansen the open-air museum in Stockholm, and to James Wilson and Nora Foster at the Swedenborg Society, who have helped in ways too numerous to mention. The photographs included in this booklet were selected from a collection taken during filming on location in Sweden and London. Some of these are to feature in forthcoming book entitled *Swedenborgs Lusthus*. A personal thanks here must go to the artist and designer James Brook for putting them in good order, and also for his skilful handling of the design and artwork for this DVD.

Photos
and
Transp.
Journal
No.4

Heaven, Hell and Other Places
a film about Emanuel Swedenborg

Written/Presented by Philip Makatrewicz
Commissioned/Produced by Stephen McNeilly
Directed/Edited by Jacob Cartwright and Nick Jordan

Script consultant: James Wilson
Publicist: Nora Foster
Photographs: Stephen McNeilly
DVD design/artwork: James Brook

Film/Booklet © 2012, The Swedenborg Society
Photographs © 2012, Stephen McNeilly

Published by:
The Swedenborg Society
Swedenborg House
20–21 Bloomsbury Way
London WC1A 2TH
United Kingdom

ISBN: 978-0-85448-173-6